Also by

Joseph P. Moris

and

Marisa P. Moris

Answers – Heaven Speaks

The Bible Speaks Series
Conversations with Jesus and the New Testament Authors

Book I Matthew and Mark

Book II Peter and John

Book III Luke and Paul

Book IV James and Jude

Book V Ask Jesus

The Bible Speaks
Conversations with Jesus and the New Testament Authors
Book VI

Jesus' 21st Century Parables

By

Joseph P Moris
Marisa P Moris

The Bible Speaks: Conversations with Jesus and the New Testament Authors

This book is dedicated to
Jesus Yeshua Christ
and all those "up there" who believe in this journey

Book VI   Jesus' 21st Century Parables

The Bible Speaks
Copyright © 2015
by
Joseph P. Moris and Marisa P. Moris
Published by Intuition Publishing

Printed in the United States of America

ISBN-10: 0-9898851-4-3
ISBN-13: 978-0-9898851-4-0

Intuition Publishing
1054 2nd Street
Encinitas, CA 92024

info@discoverintuition.com

Format and Cover by Marisa P Moris
Edited by Joseph P Moris

All rights reserved.
The contents of this book may not be reproduced in any form, except for short extracts for quotation or review, without the written permission of the publisher.
© Joseph P Moris and Marisa P Moris
First Published by Intuition Publishing
Transcriptions by Monica Harris and Lorna Mulbach
Printed in the United States of America
First Edition: November 2015

20 19 18 17 16 15 14 13 12 11 (??????)
Library of Congress Cataloging-in-Publication Data
The Bible Speaks VI
Joseph P Moris and Marisa P Moris
p.   cm.
ISBN 978-0-9898851-0-2   1.) Religion 2.) Spirituality 3.) Christianity

The Bible Speaks: Conversations with Jesus and the New Testament Authors

Ephesians 4:2-5   King James Version
Author: Paul

With all lowliness and meekness, with longsuffering, forbearing one another in love; endeavoring to keep the unity of the Spirit in the bond of peace.

There is one body, and one Spirit, even as you are called in one hope of your calling:

One Lord, One Faith, One Baptism, One God and Father of all, who is above all and through all and in you all.

Ephesians 4:2-5   As paraphrased in Heaven Speaks
by: Joseph Moris

Always be humble and gentle. Because of your love, be patient with each other, making allowance for each other's faults.

Make every effort to keep yourselves united in the Spirit, binding you together with peace.

There is one body and one Spirit, just as also, you have been called to one glorious hope for the future.

Book VI   Jesus' 21ˢᵗ Century Parables

Table of Contents

Jesus' Introduction
Introduction

I	*Parable on the Orange*
II	*Parable of the Golf Course Part 1*
III	*Parable of the Orchard*
IV	*Parable of the Dog's Toy*
V	*Parable of the Strawberry*
VI	*Parable of the Radio Station*
VII	*Parable on the Light Bulb*
VIII	*Parable of the Hologram*
IX	*Parable on the Radio and the Hard Drive*
X	*Parable of the Baby Monitor*
XI	*Parable of the Mannequin*
XII	*Parable of the Human Suit*
XIII	*Parable of the 12 Story Building*
XIV	*Parable of the Golf Course Part II*
XV	*Parable of the Orange & Parallel Universes*
XVI	*John's Parable on the Golf Course*
XVII	*Parable on the Diamond*
XVIII	*Parable of the Tennis Ball*

The Bible Speaks: Conversations with Jesus and the New Testament Authors

Jesus' Introduction

(Jesus)   .... bringing about the examples, bringing about, as they say, parables to explain to people who they are, why they are here, where they are going, where their loved ones are, where they are going in their life, are different ways they can learn to live a life in an honest fashion, but also live with the love of God within their heart, understanding and knowing that love is unconditional, love is light, light is ever withstanding to that which is darkness. So know and understand that this will be a ministerial book indeed in that people will read it to feel good. People will read it to understand. People will read it to say, 'Oh, that's what they mean. Oh, Jesus was the man, His higher self was Christ. I understand this now. Oh, this is understandable for I understand, and I understand as a man."

Introduction

Marisa and I started The Bible Speaks series in mid 2014. Throughout our interviews with the Authors of the New Testament Jesus would come in and monitor.

If you were to listen to our tapings you would hear me, Joe saying "Okay thanks Jesus but we're going to interview you at the end of these first four books for your own 'Ask Jesus' book. Well, little did I understand that Jesus was actually giving us everything we needed for the 'Ask Jesus' book which is now Book V in the Bible Speaks Series.

Included in the 'Ask Jesus' book are eighteen parables so for ease of access and carry we decided to just accumulate them together in this one small book.

The following are some great lessons from Jesus for a 21st Century world. Be aware that sometimes the parables come through Jesus' friends like Rosemary or Gabriel or Eden but they're still Jesus' lessons for all of us to learn.

I

Parable on the Orange

(Jesus)   Dear Brethren, as we convene here today and we speak of these things, you must understand that the truth lies within my heart and that as I, living as a human being, portray the things that I portray to those who followed me, they understood each of these things in their own minds as different things. For I may show each of you an orange and you may look at it and one of you may think "that's about the right size to play catch with. I'm going to throw it. It's a ball." And the other may say "I'm going to peel that and eat it." Another may say, "Oh, I'm just going to save this for later. I don't know what it is." So there are many things in the teachings in which I brought through that some people understood and some people did not, just as the teachings in which we have been giving you tonight, are things that you may or may not have understood. So in your question as you ask, there are many things in this book, in this sacred book (Bible), in the teachings in which I told, that were skewed by – not in a bad disrespectful way – skewed by those who learned it as a different way, based on their teachings or based on their experiences. Paul understood the teachings in his way. He understood these teachings and much of the information that came through.

II

Parable of the Golf Course Part 1

Marisa: I keep hearing, "I Am that I Am. I Am that I Am." Wait, here's Gabriel:

Gabriel: You speak of the I Am, and as the I Am will enter into and bring unto those the message, the message of Christ, the message of God, the "I Am that I Am" and not just the "I Am" that lies within is the one that carries with it all of the angels of God, all of the angels of God, all of the thrones of God. For the seven angels that sit amongst the shoulder, head to feet and hands of that which is God, are those that spiral through time, sending out their appreciation and love for God and bringing forth knowledge and wisdom of God. For you speak and you, Joe, ask unto us: Why is the Christ not Christed? Why is the Christ not God? Why is the Christ not within a Godhead – ?

Marisa: Oh, that's what I was obsessing about earlier. I forgot about that. Here's Gabriel:

Gabriel: And we say unto you this, for there is, there is a trail, there is a trail of Christhood unto Godhood, unto Creator, unto that which is the All That Is, the I Am that I

The Bible Speaks: Conversations with Jesus and the New Testament Authors

Am or as you say, the Elohim. The man that you call Jesus, the man that you call Jesus descends directly from the 11th dimension, the 11th dimension. For you have been looking in the 5th dimension for his presence instead of the 11th dimension. For many beings that have ascended have ascended into what you would see as a Godhead, but this in reality is only a God school. This is a soul plane unto a soul plane. So the soul plane in which you are seeing is where souls will enter new souls and they will work their way through all of the levels of incarnation and find themselves as ascended masters. They may go on through God school, or they may go off to other worlds and live amongst themselves, or they may stay on the earth plane.

For Jesus chose, Jesus chose to stay upon the earth plane, but understand and know that this is only, only a creation of the highest being, a creation of the highest being, for understand that a creation of the highest being is a creation of the highest being, for we are all creations of this, but there are beings that did not have to pass through the veil. There is one being that did not have to pass through the veil, and this is a being or a trail of light coming from Source down onto earth and all other planets; and this is where, this is where the Christs will follow this trail back up to the Creator...the Creator energy, God.

Joe: Okay, so Christ is Jesus and Jesus is God?

Gabriel: Even though he didn't want to say so...yes he is. And the reason why you do not see, why you find it so hard to understand is because he was a man and because he was a regular man, because he is just a regular man this is what brought and still brings the resonance to the earth plane an understanding and knowing that he entered into this role of God as an ascended master, but not only because he was an ascended master.

Marisa: Oh, okay. So Jesus, whose spirit at the time was an Ascended Master, became the incarnated being of God...

Joe: We talked about that a bit.

Marisa: I never believed it. I didn't believe it, because I can see it.

Joe: He jumped then – see, this is where I get some confusion, because we talked about Jesus' higher self, et cetera, but in <u>Heaven Speaks</u>, we made it clear that Jesus, the man, embodies the spirit of Christ, himself. He jumped over everything.

Marisa: Yes he did.

Joe: But then it gets confusing, because then that spirit of Jesus still had to climb up through the ranks to become Christed, so he's already Christed, because he's already God. Christ is Christ. That's all there is to it. But he also says he had to become Christed, which meant he had to go through all the various steps that it takes to eventually become Christed, to be a Creator soul. So it's still pretty confusing. To me, it's still pretty confusing, because – well, I guess the higher self is just Christ. That's all there is to it.

Marisa: Yes.

Joe: But the question is —when we started the Jesus interview, I asked: "What did you mean when on the cross you said, 'Finished at last' or 'It is done'?" It would seem to me that Christ would need to live as spirit in each one of his created beings in order to truly experience what he created.

Gabriel: And this, this you are correct, and this is — what you are saying is correct in the sense that what you must understand, what you must understand is that a perfect creation of all that is is entered upon and put upon the soul plane to enter into all of the creations in which a god has created. When the god which has created the worlds, when a god has come together and created worlds, created galaxies, yes, this Godhead in essence will want to incarnate and live within each one of its creations. It (the Godhead) will create a soul just like all the other created souls and will live through its creations, live through eternity and live through the evolving...through all the different steps of creation.

Parable of the Golf Course Part 1

It is like creating a golf course and then playing it yourself. But creating the golf course, creating all the sand traps, building the rivers and the streams, deciding what par is, deciding what type of people you're going to attract towards your course; will you be an upper-scale "professional" course or a lower-scale "municipal" course? What will this course be, and what will it represent, and how will people experience it? You will decide all of these things. You as the Godhead will then create – you as the Godhead will then create this atmosphere – (he's using atmosphere) – but the Godhead above you, the creator that creates humans, the creator that creates humans will create unique humans whereby souls will go to live in these human beings.

So let us just look at this as the golfers are the people, and you are creating souls to go live in these golfers. You as the creator of the golf course will go and live in many different golfers and experience this and see what you like about it, make tweaks, see if you need to change things or add things over a very, very long time. Then you will decide to go and be a golfer on that golf course to show everyone, show all the other golfers who have been ruining the golf course…who have been hitting the ball in the water and in the trees and never shooting par. Everyone is getting frustrated and wanting to leave or quit the game so you as God, the Creator, will enter down into one of the most experienced golfers, one of the very experienced and better golfers who has been there for a very, very, very long time and you will make a contract with their soul to incarnate through them so that you can teach others how to shoot par. They have already played this course and every course is a lifetime. They have already played this course many, many, many, many times as themselves. Yes, you were a part in creating them, so in essence, you are their creator and you created this course, and another god (Christed Being) actually created the beings that they are in, but you, you will make a contract with the soul and say, "You have these attributes. You are advanced. You will be a very good person for me to incarnate through," and then that is when God will manifest.

The Bible Speaks: Conversations with Jesus and the New Testament Authors

God will choose amongst all of the souls in which it has created and been, which it will incarnate through, and this is when God entered into Jesus when Jesus was baptized. Jesus was simply an ascended master but God incarnated and came through unto Jesus when baptized, and this is how God was able to bring the ministry and the lessons and the teachings to the world in which he had a hand at creating...or the golf course he created...by entering into Jesus. For God did not need to be a boy. God did not need to learn how to be a child. God came to teach those how to live and work through his "golf course" and how to shoot par.

Joe: We've got that golf course example in our Peter and John book.

III

Parable of the Orchard

(Jesus)   Walking upon the earth at the time that I came was like walking through an orchard. When you walk through an orchard, you see an apple tree, you see an orange tree, you see grape vines, you see blueberries, you see raspberries, you see lime trees, lemon trees. You see all of these different types of trees. Are any of them the one true tree? No. Are any of them the one true fruit? No. If you take all of them, you may end up with a fruit salad. If you walk to one tree and you say, 'Oh, this orange is delicious. I'm just going to eat oranges for the rest of my life,' this is okay too, but does it mean that the one that's eating blueberries is wrong? No. It's nurturing. It's an – it's nurture – fruit from God and nurturing from God is like nurturing with food, nurturing with fruit. Nurturing is the god. It is not the fruit you eat in order to be nurtured. So what many did not understand and still do not understand, it is the compassion and the love that you feel from God that is God. It is not the Bible, it is not the Cross, it is not the Rosary, it is not the prayer rug, it is not the – it is not the yoga stances, it is not all of the things that people think they need in order to connect with God. It is the feeling and the nourishment that one receives from quote, "God" that is inside of them that is important.

So when I came upon the earth, the earth was in great dismay in terms of religions. Many believed that they needed to kill in order for their god to forgive them. Many felt as if they needed to kill animals, others killed human beings, others had sexual sacrifices, others whipped themselves or hurt themselves to prove to God that they were unworthy so that God would love them. This is not nurturing. This is not. This is like walking into the orchard and taking a branch off the tree and whipping yourself with it and thinking that God loves you because of it. This is not the case.

So many of us from this soul pod, many of us from this soul family in which all of us are a part of, began to enter onto the earth plane to bring a message, a message of compassion, a message of love, a message of fruit, a message that when one feels nurtured, that is all that matters. When one feels the Light of God inside of them, that's all that matters. It does not matter what book, it does not matter which worshipping tools you use to get to this. It is just knowing and understanding that we are all compassionate loving beings inside of these human beasts, in essence, that we live in.

Human beings have evolved a lot since I was last – since I was alive as Yeshua Ben Joseph. Human beings have risen on the conscious level in which they carry. They can understand a lot more. The mind understands science a lot more than it did prior to this time, for when I was alive, many did not understand science. We understood astronomy to a certain extent, but did not understand science. So the reason why this soul family, our soul family is entering back into the earth at this time is because science is going to begin to prove what Constantine and his advisors put into the Bible is wrong. Science is going to start to prove this wrong.

So if we can come in and we can bring in the feeling and the nurturing of God, the nourishment of God so that all men and women on this planet can feel the nourishment of God, they will know what that is. You cannot watch a dirty movie, you cannot watch a horror movie, you cannot watch someone be hurt or abused, you cannot watch violence and feel the love of God inside of you. You may feel a perversion or an excitement if you have attachments, entity attachments, demonic attachments, even if your mind is perverted for the lack of a better word. You may feel an arousal of some sort when you see negativity, and this is just dark forces, whether it be within the mind or outside attachments. No one can legitimately and fully say that they feel the love of God when anything negative happens.

So human beings must just understand that it's the nurturing of God that's important, and this is what we brought in at this time. There are many religions, many negative religions, many positive religions, but truly, truly what we are bringing was the one true God is compassion, is love, is unconditional love, and that one true God, one true God lived inside of me, is me and is all of you, my brothers and sisters in Christ, in God."

IV

Parable of the Dog's Toy

Joe: Well, let's wrap up this evening with this final question, which is the thing we discussed earlier, we were discussing between us. I have a spirit that is within me that is my spirit, is part of my higher self, who has allowed himself to come down and be me, human, physical Joe here on earth. Was your spirit Christ? Or the Holy Ghost, the Holy Spirit?

(Jesus) My spirit was both. My spirit was both indeed. If you begin to understand the construct, the construct of the human soul, if you begin to understand the construct of this, you will see that all is one and one is all, just as many of the teachers have told you before. But understand and know that the resonance with the Holy Spirit, the resonance with the Christ consciousness, is something that every soul would like to have. Please know and understand that the Holy Spirit, so to speak, is the first physical catalyst of the god manifest. This is the first vehicle in which God consciousness traveled. This is the first vehicle in which this consciousness was able to enter into physicality in the lower dimensions.

When one can begin to comprehend that the Holy Spirit is a vehicle in which a consciousness can travel, one will begin to fully understand how it works. For, one can look at a human being, a human being with a consciousness of its own, and say the Holy Spirit is within it. But if you look at it as a Holy Spirit is what it is all in, then it begins to make a little bit more sense. So if you look at the Holy Spirit as the vehicle in which the consciousness lives in or is born into, the consciousness continues to graduate, raise its vibration, become more like the Holy Spirit, and thereby becoming Christed it will be.

Marisa: So the fact that they're saying look at the Holy Spirit as a vehicle, so the Holy Spirit is within someone –

Joe: So if you look at the Holy Spirit as a vehicle then –

(Jesus) So if you look at the Holy Spirit as the vehicle in which the consciousness lives in or is born into, the consciousness continues to graduate, raise its vibration, become more like the Holy Spirit, and thereby becoming Christed it will be. So it is that other way around that other people look at this; they look at it as an awakening, the Holy Spirit inside. Whereas, we explain to you that the Holy Spirit is the vehicle in which souls are created. Now, one can choose to turn their back on God. One can choose to not want to enter into the light. But this never changes the fact that this soul was created by the Holy Spirit.

Parable of the Dog Toy

(Jesus) Thereby look at the Holy Spirit as a little lining around the soul. It is a little lining around the soul and the soul is inside. You may look at one of your dog toys. The Holy Spirit is the fabric on the outside. The

consciousness is the stuffing. And the squeaker inside is the human being...and the human mind.

Joe: I had a feeling that one was coming. I love his analogies. I love his parables. I love his metaphors.

(Jesus) So look at the stuffing as continuing to build more and more stuffing, more stuffing with all of the things happening in that soul's life. It continues to build more and more stuffing until it is full, until it is Christed, until it has experienced all the stuffing it can possibly experience. And therefore gets rid of the squeaker, so to speak, and it then is just the Holy Spirit with the Christed soul inside. And this is how the souls evolve. When they choose to enter back into a physical body, the soul surrounds the physical body and is within the physical body. It is not that the soul is a tiny small little thing within a physical body. <u>The soul carries the physical body inside of it as well</u>.

Joe: Oh it surrounds us?

Marisa: Yes.

Joe: It is sort of our Snow Globe!

Marisa: Yes.

(Jesus) So when one is calling its soul into its heart and tuning into its soul, you may call it into your heart center to fully tune into the full capacity of the soul, but the soul is multidimensional. The soul travels through all time and space. The soul is much bigger than a physical being. A physical being is just one small, little layer of a being. So in answer to your question, each soul is already lined with the

Holy Spirit. Each soul is capable of becoming Christ. Each soul can follow in the direction of those who have become like Christ in their lifetime, Jesus being the prime example...

Marisa: This is Samuel talking now...

(Samuel)   ... Jesus being the prime example...and understanding how he did it. And this is loving your fellow man, understanding and not judging, and knowing that we are all the Holy Spirit. We are all god. And we all carry the consciousness that continues to evolve through time in order to become like Christ. And once one is like Christ, they have many choices and many worlds that they may want to go to, go to other dimensions. But for the most part, this is a graduation ceremony so to speak where the soul has accomplished its goal.

V

Parable of the Strawberry

(Jesus)   Life is like a strawberry, it is sweet, but if you do not know what it is, looking at it from the outside, you wonder what all the specks are on the outside. You wonder if you're supposed to eat the green thing on top. You wonder what it is. So you just go ahead and bite in, and that's when you see that life is sweet. So take life one day at a time, and understand that sometimes, something doesn't look the way that it is. And sometimes it's just taking that leap and understanding and knowing that there's sweetness inside, and that you may just have to avoid that green thing on top. Enjoy life, know that life is sweet. Do not be afraid to enjoy it. Do not be afraid of judgment. Just do what you love and love the sweetness in life. For the only thing that brings strife between two people is not feeling as if they are sweet enough inside and trying to protect another from them, or protect themselves from another through a reflection of what they believe is a bad heart inside. So when two begin to protect themselves against others, each other, this is the only thing that brings strife in human nature. This is the only thing. For the love that I carry is stronger than one can ever possibly imagine, and I carry this love for every one of my children.

VI

Parable of the Radio Station

(Jesus) *You must look at us as radio stations, radio stations where it does not matter how many radios are tuned into our station. It does not affect the way that we speak. It does not affect our strength. It does not affect the way that we preach or minister. We are simply here speaking, and anyone who chooses to tune into our radio station, so to speak, is able to do that. The only difference between a radio station and us is we are able to infuse you with our energy.*

VII

Parable on the Light Bulb

(Jesus) *If you look at each person as energy, you look at each person as a light bulb. You understand that one may be going dim and this is when the light bulb begins to go out for it has not had a recharge in a long time. So asking, asking I, Jesus, or the Father or the angels or the guides or the higher self to come in and recharge the light bulb will help that light bulb, that human being, see much more clearly what they need in their life.*

For we do not come in and say, "You must go left. You must go right." When we come in and we brighten the light bulb, we brighten it so that the human being may with their free will make that decision and they may be able to – and they will be able to see their higher self maybe with their – not with their eyes, but they'll be able to hear or feel or sense or get a gut feeling on what they need to do next. And this is the higher self that is directing and the higher self that knows the plan, the higher self that understands what needs to happen when the human being is on the earth plane.

VIII

Parable of the Hologram

Joe: I asked him to be with me tonight in church and to be with the pastor. Was he there tonight at church?

Marisa: He says absolutely. He says he's everywhere and nowhere all at once.

(Jesus) There is no place that you will find me and there is no place that you will not find me. If you see here

Parable of the Hologram

(Jesus) .... that what you are speaking with is a holographic image of who I am then you may look at it this way: this holographic image is just as real as I am. You may look at it like this: when one speaks in an interview on the television and they say words that are great or words that are good, this makes people happy. Therefore, the essence of that person energetically, the person speaking on the television, their energy is in fact in each one of the rooms that the people who are viewing the television have. So please try to see it that way. When a Christian calls in, or anyone calls in, Christ, Jesus, me, they are simply turning the TV on so they may feel and hear the words in which I am speaking, and in doing this subconsciously they are becoming protected, raising their vibration (and) therefore

negativity cannot get through and the negative spirit realm cannot get through. For the spirit realm is very tricky and many a times it's warred against. There are many people that misuse this. But understanding that we are spirits living here, understanding that we are spirits living here is something that is much greater than many people understand or believe, and this is why we come with ministries to teach people that they can do just as much or more than I ever displayed 2,000 years ago.

IX

Parable of the Radio and Hard Drive

Joe: *I sure am glad Jesus can be everywhere at the same time. I feel so guilty taking his time.*

(Jesus) *Why do you feel guilty?*

Joe: *I don't know. I'm thinking of the church today and they brought up that story again how everyone wants your attention... how in the world can you accommodate everyone that wants your attention at the same time?*

(Jesus) *I am in each human being. Everything that I have ever done and everything that I will ever do is stored within your body and within your soul and it is too hard for some human minds to understand this, but this is stored within you. For there is no time, there is no time on this side so everything is happening at once. And by each person having a piece of me inside of them, every single person has a copy of that which they may access at any time.*

Joe: *So we have you inside of us, and inside of you is the Holy Spirit? Or is the Holy Spirit separate and you separate inside of me?.... plus my spirit too? It's kind of crowded inside there.*

Marisa: *There are a lot of heavenly bodies inside us.*

Joe: There's you and there's......

Marisa: There is the physical body and there are all the energetic bodies. Humankind knows of 12, but there are several more. There are 67 in fact. And these all carry out into different pieces of the universe and they each carry information......Here is Eden (One of Joe's Guides)....

(Eden) They each carry information that is pertinent to living a lifetime on the earth plane or other physical planes. As you learn to develop each one of these bodies and as you begin to learn to communicate with these bodies, you see that, we see that, and we try to have the world see that, we are all one. This word is used... this term is used so loosely. People say "we are all one, we are all one, we do not disintegrate, we stand together, we are all one," but nobody truly gets the understanding that we really are all one. Because we each are all made of the same thing and what we are made of, we have that inside of us, that pure peace inside of us, just as a daughter has her father's energy within her, if she was able to communicate with that energy, then that daughter would be able to know everything that he knew. This is a lot of the information that is stored in DNA. But human beings are only first starting to begin to understand DNA.

Marisa: Here's Jesus with another parable ....

Parable of the Radio and the Hard Drive

(Jesus) So in saying that the Holy Spirit is in each person, you may look at that as one little two-way radio. You look at the Christ light as another little radio. You can look at the human spirit as another radio. You can look at

the soul, the over soul, you can look at the guides, all as different radios, and when one wants to communicate with one of these things, the radio buzzes the spirit incarnation in which they want to communicate with, and that spirit talks, therefore the vibration is affected by the person who is asking for help. And in asking for help, each person could ask 15 different questions and everybody would get a different answer at the same time. For if everything you knew, Joe, if every single thing you knew was on a hard drive, so to speak, if everything you ever knew and everything you ever will know, and people had a key to that hard drive stored inside of them, that they could access at any time, just by asking a question, they would receive an answer from the abundant amount of information that is stored within your hard drive. Does this make sense?

Joe: Sort of. So, basically Jesus is comparing himself to like a hard drive but we're not really smart enough yet to know how to tap into all of that knowledge?

Marisa: Yes. Here is Eden. She wants to clarify ....

(Eden)   As the world evolves into the fourth and higher dimensions, everybody will be able to communicate with that divine piece inside of them, and that is why many other planets have the ability to tap into this divine piece inside of them and therefore they remember who they are. They incarnate only to develop their abilities, to live in different places, to learn from the people, to learn different healing modalities, different cultures, but living on the earth plane you're correct, many do not have the ability to accept that they have Christ within them, even if they are a Christian.

The Bible Speaks: Conversations with Jesus and the New Testament Authors

Joe: Jesus has said that 85% of self-proclaimed Christians are really skeptical and find it hard to believe in him because in today's world of science coupled with a 2000 year old and hard to understand Bible, Christians find it hard to put trust in something and someone they can't see or hear.

Marisa: I'm glad I can see and hear him.

Joe: You're lucky!

X

Parable of the Baby Monitor

Joe: So no one is ever alone?

(Jesus) You may look at it like a baby sleeping with a baby monitor. The baby is sleeping and everything is fine. Nobody worries. But they hear the baby cry and they go run. They don't just run to the monitor. They run to the room. So look at it like that. Know that each person is protected but they are not spied on, or watched. Each person has access to an army of angels and because each person has the knowledge of Christ, the knowledge of the Holy Spirit within their body, technically we are all mini gods, so to speak, because we have access to that information and we can co-create with the divine creator a life that we desire and in that comes the ability to connect to those that we love on one side or another. So in answer to your question, it depends on what each soul has decided they want to do. If one goes to a concert and they choose "I'm going to take three friends with me so that I don't get lost within this crowd" and another says, "I'm just going to go with one person" or "I'm going to go by myself but I have my cell phone just in case something happens, I can call someone." So everybody is completely different. So for the most part, each person has anywhere between 5-7 teachers, guides or family members that are with them at all times and this includes angels.

Joe: Whoa....okay....so like when I went to church tonight I'm going to guess there's lots and lots and lots of teachers, guides, angels, family members, etcetera in the church with us tonight then....

(Jesus) Absolutely. You can look at it like this. You can look at it as they are actually on the earth plane, or they are communicating through the telephone. There are many times where family members including your mother or your father, will come in and technically they are somewhere else, but they are dialing in.... technically they are calling in from another place. You are seeing them just like a photograph telephone. You are seeing the words in action and they are becoming a manifestation of those words. There are other times where we actually come to the earth plane and that can be itself much greater, with the ringing of the ears, the tapping of the head, the chills on the body. Many times this is when we make our entrance into the earth plane. But yes, in church, there are many who are receiving downloads, so to speak, information from their higher self. The higher self is always receiving information from the guides from this side.

XI

Parable of the Mannequin

Joe: Has the Holy Spirit always been within mankind? And why was it so – why does the Bible make it seem like the Holy Spirit did not exist until the day of Pentecost which was the resurrection of Jesus?

(Jesus) The way that men see things, the way that man sees things in general is that things are on the outside and brought to the inside and being activated. They do not look at it as.... look at it like this ....

Parable of the Mannequin

(Jesus) Inside the human body ... look at the human body as a hollow mannequin. Imagine that there are many light bulbs inside of that mannequin. There are many things. And, there's a light bulb that symbolizes the Holy Spirit. When this light bulb is turned on or activated, this light shines brightly and it fills the entire mannequin; this light begins shooting out of the mannequin's head and out of the mannequin's feet, therefore connecting this mannequin to the Divine, to the Divine as to Mother Earth.

By understanding that when one is connected in these ways then the vibration in which they have is raised. The higher the vibration of a human being and the etheric subtle and energetic bodies that this spirit is residing in, or this consciousness resides in, the higher the vibration, the more quote-unquote "spiritual abilities" one will have. These are called spiritual abilities because these are all things that spirits can do even when in a human body. But when they say that the Holy Spirit comes to – comes to – a man, they are in essence saying that the mannequin does not have the light bulb in there to begin with, and somebody comes and puts it in the mannequin. This is not the case. It is there and it is activated. It is activated indeed. The switch has just not been turned on.

So when one turns that switch on of, as they say, the Holy Spirit, or one turns on that switch of the 'I Am', or the 'I Am Divine', or the 'I Am God'....when they turn that belief on and understand that they are the true co-creator with the Creator of their life, the vibration that they carry raises. Heaviness falls away. And yes, spiritual abilities are developed. Does this answer the question?

Joe: Yeah. I love his examples... his parables. Okay, so I'm picturing that people just didn't realize they had the Holy Spirit within them until Jesus said to them: "I am going to give you the Spirit of Truth and that will be your helper." And the spirit of truth therefore is my angel light bulb within.

(Jesus)   The Spirit of Truth is technically what people, man, call the Holy Spirit. The Spirit of Truth is within each and every person. And just as we have spoken in many other sittings that we have had, we have mentioned the hollowed out tennis balls (example is found with interviews with Matthew, Mark and Luke).

We have mentioned these because each one represents a different layer, a different aspect, a different piece of that human being. So if you look at the totality of the consciousness of what a spirit really contains, you can look at that mannequin and you can look at that light bulb, and technically that is the Holy Spirit, but there may be another bigger light bulb on the outside of it that is the soul's personality, another light bulb that is the spirit personality, and a big huge light bulb up in the mannequin's head with a big, red beaming light, that is the intellectual mind and it says "I am you, I am you, I am you," with strobe lights and red lights going off. And only until the consciousness of that mannequin -- which lies in the belly and in the heart -- as their consciousness realize that the big red flashing thing in their head is technically just a tool they may turn that off and allow the white light inside of them to take over the consciousness.

XII

Parable of the Human Suit

Joe: That's great. I love it. And, I'll talk to Peter, when we have a chance to talk to Peter again....

Marisa: Here is Peter again on the "human clothing" the "human suit"...

Parable of the Human Suit

(Peter) And when we say that the Holy Spirit is within each person, many people call the Holy Spirit different things. You call it the Holy Spirit. We call it the Light. We call it the Eternal. We call it the Alpha, the Omega. We call it the Infinite. So understanding that the brightest possible light that can be placed within a human being is that of the Holy Spirit, as you call it, that each person has this divine fire, this divine flame inside and it is ready to be activated. It does not have to be through, as humans say, Christianity. It does not have to be through a certain religion. This can be done through meditation or prayer. This can be done through self-affirmation. This can be done through the realization that you are a divine being living in a human suit.

You are living in a body and this body is like clothing that talks. And as you begin to see that this clothing is talking you realize the talking clothing is not you. It is something you are wearing. And as you and other human beings become aware that this talking clothing really doesn't know much of what it's saying, and you begin to realize that it is just your clothing talking, that is when the vibration raises. That is when one begins to realize "I am a spirit. I am God. I am love, and I am ascending into Christhood just as many others have with the help of those like me who have ascended as well."

Marisa: *I picture a bunch of talking clothes.*

Joe: *How do they come up with this stuff?*

XIII

Parable of the 12 Story Building

(Jesus) When the angelic kingdom reigned upon the third dimensional world they were hoping to bring this into a world where they could incarnate on a regular basis for they were only living in the fifth, sixth, seventh, and eighth worlds. They were not living in the lower world. And they wanted to have a physical experience. Whereby, this is what they did. This is what they did indeed in hoping to create their own world, their own world, for there were many, many that got wrapped into that which is the Luciferian rebellion in that one with much power decided that they did not want to do what the plan was. They wanted to mix it up. And this was a good idea to many, this was a good idea indeed to many, except for the ones that did not think that it was a good idea.

So understand that it was all done in good intentions and there are still those who believe that it was done with good intentions. They are still from the belief that there should be no reason why we have to evolve into combining with our higher self, combining with our spirit, combining with our soul and losing our individuality. There are those who believe that they want to be their individual self for eternity. And this is understandable in that we have free will. So know that the ones that are walking in the light, so to speak, are those who want to rejoin their consciousness *with a group and lose their individuality and no longer be themselves.*

(Jesus) When I say that some believed it to be a good idea, I do not rebuke this comment for there are many on the earth plane and many in the celestial realms and in the ethers that believe different things. What one must understand, what one must understand indeed is that, there are different beings at different levels of consciousness and when I speak of those who do not want to re-emerge, re-emerge with their higher self, I must explain this in a fashion in which you can understand.

Parable of the 12 Story Building

(Jesus) For, when you look at a building, you look at a building, and you look at a building with 12 stories, you say "this is a person." So the building is a person. The person is not each floor. For if you look at the spirit being, the spirit being is the second floor and you look at the human being is the first floor. So when somebody says "I want to be the second floor forever. I want to be the second floor forever. I want to be my spirit forever and I want to live on the second floor forever," they are blind to the fact that they are already living on every single floor because they are the building. So when we say the spirit merges with the higher self, this is not truly, truly the way that it happens, for what happens is the awareness, the awareness of one's self begins to evolve just as we have talked prior to this about human beings deciding which consciousness, which level of awareness they want to plug into, so to speak.

So, when we say this, we say this as there are many who get caught up in the illusion, the illusion that there are all these different floors in the building and forget that they are the building. They are the building. And by being the building they are still the first floor, the second floor, the third floor, the fourth floor. But the Luciferian rebellion is telling those that are on the second floor experiencing second floor life, saying, "Why would you ever want to be a third floor or a fourth floor or a fifth floor? Why would you ever want to do that? You would never be a second floor again." And so these aspects, these aspects of these buildings, these floors within these buildings, get caught up in being afraid that they are going to lose an entire segment of themselves. So when you look at yourself even by saying "Joe, when will I ever graduate to be my higher self?" You already are your higher self.

So as you begin to see that you are your higher self, and there are different aspects of you, different aspects of you that come into play at times, for Joe the human being is the first floor, and you may call up to the fifth floor and get some information, and you may call up to the second floor and get some information, up to the third floor and get some information, and get information from many different aspects of yourself, many different aspects of yourself, but it does not mean that you are not also those aspects. For what we must explain is sometimes the illusion is much more fun to souls than the real thing. For, the illusion, the illusion that we are separate, that we are separate from God is the game, is the game that we play. And we do not say it is a game because we belittle it. It is a game because it is something that people look at games as something that they want to win, they want to beat, they want to master.

XIV

Parable of the Golf Course Part II

(Jesus)   You look at your game of golf, Joe, look at each incarnation; each incarnation is a different day on the golf course. You will say, "Ooh, ooh, I got a bogie on hole 3 and I hit it into the water and had to take an extra stroke. Next time I'm going to hit it a little bit to the left and that way it won't go in the water." And that's what you say in between games. And then the next game comes along and you're talking to your buddies, you're talking to your friends, and "oops" there it goes in the water again. You say, "Oh next time I'm not going to hit it in the water. I'm not going to hit it in the water." And look, there it goes in the water again. And that is how incarnation is over and over, the same mistakes, the same habits each soul has. Each soul has habit after habit and it's because of their energetic habits programming within yourself that says "must hit ball in water, must hit ball in water and take extra stroke" until one can realize, realize this is a game. I'm not programmed. I don't have to be programmed to hit it that way and I can say, "You know what? Even though I really want to hit it that way, I'm just going to hit it the other way."

So you must look at each incarnation and then also realize that when you go to hit that ball, you have up to 12 people standing behind you at any given time going, "Hey, hit to the left. Hit to the left. Don't hit it in the water." And it's your choice to choose if you want to hit the ball in the water or hit it the other way this time. So look at this life, this life on the earth plane as yes, there are the evils, there is the water where the ball can go into, but what fun would the game be without the sand traps and the water? This is the way that we look at the world. There must be something that defers us from the good, so to speak, to make it a challenge to stay within the good. And yes, there is suffering. Yes, there is violence. Yes there is anger. Yes there are many, many horrible, horrible things that souls must endure as human beings, but we all must remember that as souls living in human bodies, yes, humans are very real, humans are very real. But for souls we do not die. We live forever. We live forever. So, yes, there are horrible things happening, but there are many, many, many things to learn from these horrible things happening.

For if we were to place the world on a pedestal and say "there shall be no evil," souls would not want to incarnate here because they would get bored, they would not grow, they would not expand, they would not learn the amount that they would want to learn. So what you must see this as is a game; a very serious game. And each soul does not look at this like school. Each soul looks at this as a round of golf and says, "Next time I'm going to do better. Next time I'm going to get par. Next time I'm going to get a birdie. Next time..." And it's a challenge, and it's fun. And when they realize that they have the caddie and they realize that they have their buddies there that they couldn't see before that are helping them through to tell them which way to hit the ball, and how fast the wind is blowing, and which way to go, and which club to use, that is when, that is when the game gets really fun because no one else knows they have a caddie and no one else knows that they have someone to tell them which club to use.

So it's almost like there is a cheat sheet. And this is what I brought in. This is what I brought in as Jesus, as Jesus. I brought in the cheat sheet, the understanding that there is something inside that will direct you and tell you which way to go. And for those, those who get so angry at religion, they turn away from the fact that they have this help, that they have these angels, that they have this guidance, that they have this with them, that they have the whole course map right at their fingertips but they do not see this because they are trapped on the second floor, so to speak. They are trapped in the illusion that they are only one floor of their building. It would be like saying, "Hi, I am Joe," but it is only your leg speaking. It would be like your leg thinking that it is Joe. Or it would be like your hand thinking that it is Joe or even your brain thinking, "Hi, I am Joe." No, that's not the case. That's not the case. You are Joe. The whole vehicle is Joe. And your consciousness lives inside, and depending on which floor you choose to live on, that is the frequency, that is the consciousness and the awareness and the understanding of the universe that you bring in. If you choose to live on the top floor, this is your higher self, your soul, the highest possible piece of you, and you bring in, you bring in oneness. You bring in oneness. And this I say.

XV

Parable of the Orange and the Parallel Universes

(Jesus)   Think of the earth as an orange so that you can understand that it is supple and ripe and ready to create in itself another earth, and when this earth carbon copies itself into another dimension, we will begin to see that everything that is happening here is also happening there, and our consciousness is able to go from this over to that.

It is very hard for a human mind to understand and it is very hard for us to explain to you something that the mind cannot even fathom. But imagine this, you are on an experiment. You're in an experiment. And from that experiment come 11 other mirrored worlds that have the exact same thing happening but the consciousness is different so different things are played out in different ways. Whereby you see somebody walk in to get a job and here they are unhappy that they receive the job. On the other world they are excited that they got the job. The same things are happening, it is just different emotions, and when you see that, the difference between third dimensional and fourth dimensional and fifth dimensional emotional levels, you see that even though the life is exactly the same, it is lived completely different and it is experienced by the higher self and the essence of that which is the soul in many different ways.

For the spirit or the soul does not just experience three dimensional lives. The spirit is experiencing all dimensions in all worlds in all parallel universes in all realities in all ways of possibly doing something. For there is another world where you went left in this one, you went right in the other, and the essence of that which is your soul is experiencing that as well. So by excluding your soul, excluding the spirit, excluding the higher self from that which is your consciousness you are truly, truly not experiencing life at all. Whereby bringing in energies and knowledge from the higher dimensional "Yous" you are able to bring in knowledge that you would not have in this one due to the emotional stability of most human beings

XVI

John's Parable of the Golf Course

Joe: What the heck are the horses in Revelation?

(John)   When we speak of the horses we speak of frequencies, we speak of, just as we have spoken of the barbed wire fence in the last conversations we've had, we speak of the barbed wire fence, we speak of different frequencies, we speak of different types of music so to speak that will activate different things. When we speak of the seals, we speak of the things that are broken within the human body, mind, and spirit that are able to begin to allow the spirit to ascend to higher aspects of its self. For Jesus was able to ascend through all seven of the energy bodies within man while in a human body, therefore becoming Christed.

When I speak of the lamb and the councils or the head of these souls bowing before the lamb, it is showing the gratitude that shows that a spirit or a personality has actually made it through, ascended, and become Christed within a world where no one had ever done this. For these 12 souls that created this planet were waiting upon someone to complete this, someone to break the seal; someone to say it is doable, it is passable.

John's Parable of the Golf Course

(John)   Think of a game. Think of a game, Joe. You and 11 other souls create a golf course that seems very tough, there are very tough encounters to go through, but one golfer makes it, they pass, they pass, they make it through, and they get par on every single hole through storms, through desert weather, through shining sun, through sleet, through hail, and they make it through and this brings a celebration. This brings a celebration unto these 12 souls that have created this very difficult golf course for there are others who are trying to defeat (those trying to complete the golf course). There are others that are standing in front of the golfers. There are others that are playing very loud music behind the golfer when they are trying to concentrate and trying to make it through this golf course that you and the 11 other souls have created. For you are councils over this but you cannot really do much other than watch and wait as you have created this golf course, you have created these golfers to make it through this course quite perfectly. So when one makes it and makes it through, they are the lamb, they are Christed, and it breaks the seal, and says unto everybody else that is wandering this golf course that, "You can do this too!"

"And guess what, we are going to send help. We are going to send this music or these frequencies through this barbed wire fence that surrounds your golf course, and this will cause everybody to want to hit birdies (one under par). This will tell everybody to focus. This will tell everybody to turn their loud music off so that each person can concentrate while they are trying to hit the ball."

The Bible Speaks: Conversations with Jesus and the New Testament Authors

So understand and know that these horses are bringing help to the people of earth. The horses and the seals signify and represent the different chakras within the body of each human being that lives. For each human being has a root chakra and this root chakra brings foundation, it brings the home, it brings the security, it brings family, it brings all of the things that a child between the ages of zero and six need. For you see a child that is grasping for their parent's hand. They are developing their root chakra. There are many human beings that have never made it past this. All they worry about is their home. All they worry about is their car. All they worry about is their security. They do not have emotions, human emotions. For their spirit is kept within the root.

For when we bring peace unto this earth, this will bring peace unto these people so that they may begin to move up to the second seal, which is the emotional body. And understand that they will begin to understand and learn emotions. For a spirit to ascend into an ascended master as they call it, and eventually become Christed, they must experience life with all of their seven seals activated.

Joe: That's good because we've still got more seals and horses to go through. Alright, we've gotten through the white horse that wins many battles and gains the victory.

XVII

Parable of the Diamond

Marisa: *Okay, so let's see – oh, I didn't finish the prayer. Let's see here. Okay. Someone named Rosemary is here from the Bible. I don't know this Rosemary. She said she lived back then. She had a tough childhood.*

(Rosemary)   Jesus told me the demons weren't placed on there by God, that they are placed on there by man; that there were demons around men and the only way to stay away from the demons was to trust in the Father and trust in the Father's love to surround, to surround us all. He gave us a simple parable. He compared us, he compared us to, as we have said, the salt of the earth, but he also compared us to a piece of coal and a stone. He said, "Look at the stone. Look at the crystal, the crystal and the stone –

Marisa: Hold on. She's showing me something. No it's not a crystal it's a....

Parable of the Diamond

(Rosemary)   .... a diamond." He compared us to a diamond and he said the coal is around the diamond and the spirit is inside, and when this coal can fall off then the diamond can show, but if we take the pressure and the love of the unconditional love that is carried within that of the

Christ, we will then become Christed one day and this love will just "poof" remove the coal.

Joe: To reveal the diamond....

(Rosemary) To reveal the diamond so that we feel like the diamond and we shine like the diamond and we are the diamond, and this is what I carried with me as I felt like the diamond. I released the coal and I released the demons, and this is something that I was forever grateful for and I will be forever grateful for and I will continue to teach his words and I will stay on the earth plane in this time, in this space to help the evolution of the planet, because people do not understand or put behind the teachings the excitement and the joy and the effervescent love that is expanding throughout the world.

XVIII

Parable of the Tennis Ball

Marisa: Here's Rosemary channeling Jesus.

(Rosemary) Just look at the spirit, or the soul or the higher self as the higher piece of you and understand that within that piece of you imagine a tennis ball cut in half and that tennis ball inside of it has a smaller tennis ball that fits perfectly in it. So there is a little rim inside and then another smaller tennis ball and another smaller tennis ball and then a small and small and smaller all the way down. If you look at that as your higher self, your spirit, your soul for each layer, if you look at that as the Christ within you, this covers everything and this is what Jesus taught.

Joseph: Oh, that is nice and easy.

(Rosemary) If you look at this, look at every single aspect. For when you ask, I heard earlier when you asked, when am I able to talk to my soul? You can talk to your soul right now. You can talk to your soul. You can talk to your soul group, you can talk to your over-soul, you can talk to Christ and you can talk to God whether you can hear them back, that is a different story. We are much easier to hear as we have incarnated as guides and we are easier to hear at times than words directly from God. But God sends these messages with angels. With angels many a time, so you will get the messages regardless. But please look at that piece of God inside of you. It is a multi-layered ball and when you utilize

that you do not need to differentiate between, I'm calling my spirit, I'm calling my higher self, I'm calling my soul, oh wait no, no, I need to call in Christ or wake the over-soul!

Marisa: *She's being exuberant. She is making fun of it (how we pray).*

Joseph: *Ha, ha, ha. That is okay. I don't mind.*

(Rosemary) Well what we need to do is to understand that all of these levels are God and you are God just as I am God, but I understand that Eden just said, "You know what Rosemary, they need to understand it that way otherwise they are not going to understand. (Eden is one of Joseph's guides)

Marisa: *Eden is getting all... not defensive, but just kind of like...*

(Rosemary) It may have been easy for you to understand when you are there because the consciousness was lower to just go okay God, but Eden is saying that there are a lot of people on the Earth-plane right now that need to understand the hierarchy because they will understand how they were created and where they came from.

Joseph: *Well we did the foundation in our first book I think.*

Marisa: *Yeah.*

Joseph: *I mean it is not a perfect book, but the foundation is there.*

Marisa: *Yeah, the book is good.*

Joseph: *I know, I don't want any negativity in this at all.*

Book VI   Jesus' 21st Century Parables

(Eden)   There won't be any negativity but we must share with you the exact information so that you may understand how to place the information so that it is correct, but not negative for we do not want to draw any Christians, true Christians away from Christianity. But there will be a world with no religion in the near future. Within the next few hundred years, religion will not exist. Religion is laws. Religion is government. Religion is power, control and undermining the human being of what they are capable of. And assigning people who are Godlier than another because they say they are and having people go to that person in order to connect with God when God is as Rosemary said a tennis ball surrounded by another tennis ball and another tennis ball inside, in layers like an onion and when that piece of God inside is resonated with and spoken to it speaks back. For do not look at God as outside of you, look at God as something somewhere everywhere and the inside of that tennis ball has a walkie-talkie, and this walkie-talkie communicates directly with God wherever God may be. So technically, listening to the inside of you is where you are getting the information, not from the outside, so this must be understood as well and as soon as people can understand that God does not judge, you do not need to go to another human being in order to connect with God, the world will be a completely different place, and this is what we look forward to.

Authors Page

Joseph Patrick Moris Marisa Patrice Moris and Poochi

Joseph P. Moris is an author and columnist. Joe co-authored with his daughter Marisa their first book entitled: "*Answers: Heaven Speaks*." Joe also writes a lifestyle column for the North Coastal San Diego County newspaper "*The Coast News*" and is currently a semi-retired real estate broker/owner for *Coastal Country Real Estate* in Encinitas, CA and living part-time in Puerto Vallarta and also Playa Los Cocos near San Blas in mainland Mexico. Joe also studied and earned Bachelor Degrees in 1977 in Political Science and Economics at the University of California, Santa Barbara. He is also a US Army veteran of the Vietnam War era.

Marisa P. Moris is the founder and director of *Discover Intuition*. Marisa co-authored, with her father Joe, "Answers: Heaven Speaks." She is a teacher, a spiritual intuitive and "clairvoyant channel" who helps her clients find their true inner spiritual self and yet….so much more!

Marisa has also co-authored the Skeptic series of books dealing with subjects such as the Universe, Intuition, Tao, Reincarnation, Creation Physics, and much more with author/publisher/film maker William Gladstone.

www.ingramcontent.com/pod-product-compliance
Lightning Source LLC
Chambersburg PA
CBHW070501050426
42449CB00012B/3070